Modern Publishing
A Division of Unisystems, Inc.
New York, New York 10022
Printed in Italy

Fisher-Price

Counting Rhymes

Modern Publishing
A Division of Unisystems, Inc.
New York, New York 10022
Series UPC #: 39640

Let's learn about numbers.
Once we've begun,
You're sure to discover
That counting is fun!

To every riddle,
A number's the key.
If you want the answer,
You can count on me!

My question's easy,
I'm sure you'll agree:
How many horns
Do you see on me?

If you start to count,
You'll soon be done.
It doesn't take long
When the answer's **1**.

Next comes the walrus.
I'm very cool.
I love to play
In my swimming pool.

My tusks are the finest
You'll find in the zoo.
Can you help me count them?
You're right: there are **2**!

For laziness
I've won renown.
My world looks better
Upside down.

I am a sloth.
I live in a tree.
I hang by my toes.
How many? **3**.

I'm man's best friend,
And woman's, too.
I love to walk
And play with you.

Fetching your slippers
Is hardly a chore.
You've only got two feet.
I've got **4**.

I am a moose.
I'm big and strong.
A shady forest
Is where I belong.

I'm proud of my antlers.
They help me survive.
Can you count the points on each one?
There are **5**.

I live on the beach
In my hard, pretty shell.
My claws are quite sharp,
And they pinch very well.

I always crawl sideways.
My legs are like sticks.
How many do I need
To scuttle? All **6**.

I am a peacock.
I'm pretty and vain.
I strut around proudly
In sunshine or rain.

My tail is my pride,
With its pretty blue eyes.
If you can count **7**,
Then you win the prize.

Now don't be surprised
When you count up my arms.
Octopuses have many.
It's one of our charms.

For hugging and juggling,
My arms are first rate.
How many are there?
The total is **8**.

My neck comes in handy
For reaching up high.
The tastiest leaves
I pluck down from the sky.

Now back to our numbers.
You count while I dine.
How many spots do I have?
There are **9**.

I count on my fingers,
Or sometimes my toes.
I have the same number,
As everyone knows.

I'll hold up my fingers,
You count them, and then,
You'll certainly tell me
The answer is **10**.

Say all of the numbers,
And when you are done,
Try saying them backwards,
From **10** down to **1**.